Victorian Fa
& Posies
IN CROSS STITCH
Jane Alford

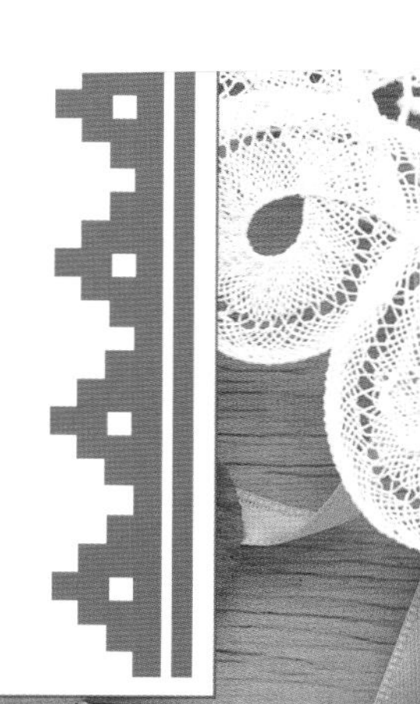

MEREHURST

THE CHARTS

Some of the designs in this book are very detailed and, due to inevitable space limitations, the charts may be shown on a comparatively small scale; in such cases, readers may find it helpful to have the particular chart with which they are currently working enlarged.

THREADS

The projects in this book were all stitched with DMC stranded cotton embroidery threads. The keys given with each chart also list thread combinations for those who wish to use Anchor or Madeira embroidery threads. It should be pointed out that the shades produced by different companies vary slightly, and it is not always possible to find identical colours in a different range.

Published in 1999 by Merehurst Limited
Ferry House, 51-57 Lacy Road, Putney, London SW15 1PR

ISBN 1 85391 764 8

A catalogue record for this book is available from the British Library.

Editor: Heather Dewhurst
Designer: Maggie Aldred
Photographer: Juliet Piddington
Illustrators: King & King Design Associates and John Hutchinson
Senior Commissioning Editor: Karen Hemingway
CEO and Publisher: Anne Wilson
International Sales Director: Mark Newman
Colour separation by Bright Arts (H K) Ltd
Printed in Hong Kong by Wing King Tong

CONTENTS

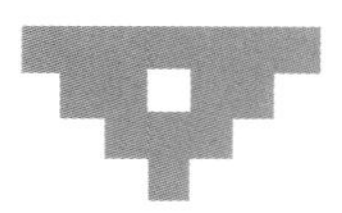

Introduction

Many of the designs in this book are based on the original Berlin woolwork designs, which were popular during the 19th century. Undoubtedly, the most attractive charts produced in Germany were those of flowers. These were very detailed and accurate reproductions of the actual flowers and took hours to reproduce because they were hand-painted. This type of design appealed to the Victorians because of its richness which, combined with the Victorian love of adornment, resulted in some beautiful pieces of embroidery.

The Victorian love of fans is reflected in several of the designs in this collection, from the violet fan with its delicate lacy background and gold border, to the beautiful fan-shaped box, richly embellished with beads and metallic thread. Tiny beads have also been used to embroider the bows of the floral trio and the lily and violet picture; when combined with metallic thread, they produce a sumptuous effect.

Jewellery was very important to the Victorians and this has not been forgotten in these designs. The exquisite brooches and picture worked on evenweave linen capture the very essence of this period. Perforated paper has been used to create two attractive greetings cards. Cards such as these were very popular during the 19th century and often contained messages of endearment.

I hope that, as you browse through the book, you find many projects you will like to stitch and that you enjoy the finished results!

Basic Skills

BEFORE YOU BEGIN

PREPARING THE FABRIC

Even with an average amount of handling, many evenweave fabrics tend to fray at the edges, so it is a good idea to overcast the raw edges, using ordinary sewing thread, before you begin.

FABRIC

Most of the projects in this book use Aida fabric, which is ideal both for beginners and more advanced stitchers as it has a surface of clearly designated squares, each cross stitch being worked over a square. Other projects use evenweave fabrics, which have 28 or 27 threads per 2.5cm (1in) each way, but in these cases the stitches are worked over two threads.

All evenweaves have a count, referring to the number of Aida blocks, threads or perforations, per 2.5cm (1in) in each direction. The lower the count, therefore, the larger the finished stitching. If you wish to use fabric with a different stitch count, count the maximum number of stitches on the chart horizontally and vertically and divide these numbers by the stitch count of your chosen fabric; this will give you the dimensions of the design when stitched on your fabric.

THE INSTRUCTIONS

Each project begins with a full list of the materials that you will require. The measurements given for the embroidery fabric include a minimum of 5cm (2in) all around to allow for preparing the edges to prevent them from fraying.

Colour keys for stranded embroidery cottons — DMC, Anchor or Madeira — are given with each chart. It is assumed that you will need to buy one skein of each colour mentioned in a particular key, even though you may use less.

In some instances, only very short lengths of thread are used: perhaps a couple of stitches in white to highlight eyes, or dots of yellow for flower centres. For this reason, if you intend to stitch cards for your friends on a fairly regular basis, it would be useful to have threads in a few standard colours.

Where metallic threads have been used, the specific make of thread is listed, without giving any equivalent. Several manufacturers produce these threads, but each brand will vary significantly, and it is not always possible to find a close equivalent. If you are unable to obtain the named thread, you may be able to substitute a similar thread for an equally attractive, if perhaps slightly different, effect, but you should experiment to ensure that you achieve a good coverage of the fabric before using it in your finished embroidery.

Before you begin to embroider, always mark the centre of the design with two lines of basting stitches, one vertical and one horizontal, running from edge to edge of the fabric (to find the centre on the chart, count the maximum number of stitches each way and divide by two).

As you stitch, use the centre lines given on the chart and the basting threads on your fabric as reference points for counting the squares and threads to position your design accurately.

WORKING IN A HOOP

A hoop is the most popular frame for use with small areas of embroidery. It consists of two rings, one fitted inside the other; the outer ring usually has an adjustable screw attachment so that it can be tightened to hold the stretched fabric in place. Hoops are available in several sizes, ranging from 10cm (4in) in diameter to quilting hoops with a diameter of 38cm (15in). Hoops with table stands or floor stands attached are also available.

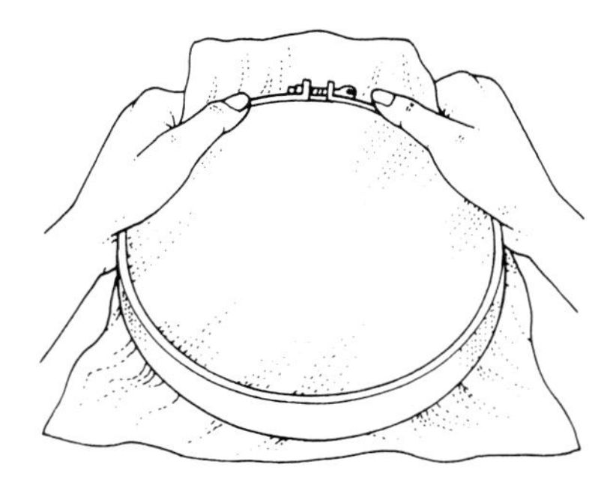

1 To stretch your fabric in a hoop, place the area to be embroidered over the inner ring and press the outer ring over it, with the tension screw released. Tissue paper can be placed between the outer ring and the embroidery, so that the hoop does not mark the fabric. Lay the tissue paper over the fabric when you set it in the hoop, then tear away the central embroidery area.

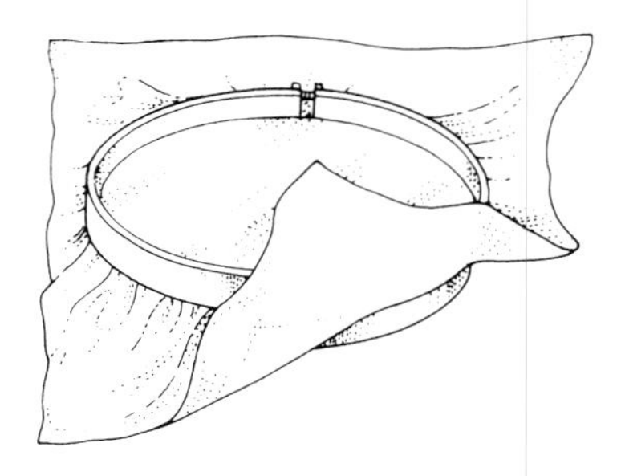

2 Smooth the fabric and, if necessary, straighten the grain before tightening the screw. The fabric should be evenly stretched.

WORKING IN A RECTANGULAR FRAME

Rectangular frames are more suitable for larger pieces of embroidery. They consist of two rollers, with tapes attached, and two flat side pieces, which slot into the rollers and are held in place by pegs or screw attachments. Available in different sizes, either alone or with adjustable table or floor stands, frames are measured by the length of the roller tape, and range in size from 30cm (12in) to 68cm (27in). As alternatives to a slate frame, canvas stretchers and the backs of old picture frames can be used. Provided there is sufficient extra fabric around the finished size of the embroidery, the edges can be turned under and simply attached with drawing pins (thumb tacks) or staples.

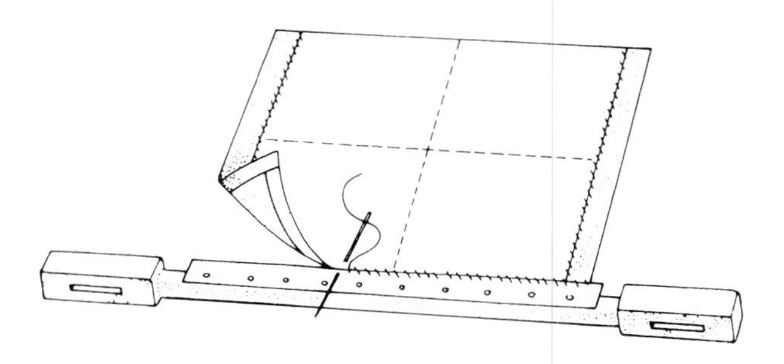

1 To stretch your fabric in a rectangular frame, cut out the fabric, allowing at least an extra 5cm (2in) all around the finished size of the embroidery. Baste a single 12mm (1/2in) turning on the top and bottom edges and oversew strong tape, 2.5cm (1in) wide, to the other two sides. Mark the centre line both ways with basting stitches. Working from the centre outwards and using strong thread, oversew the top and bottom edges to the roller tapes. Fit the side pieces into the slots and roll any extra fabric on one roller until the fabric is taut.

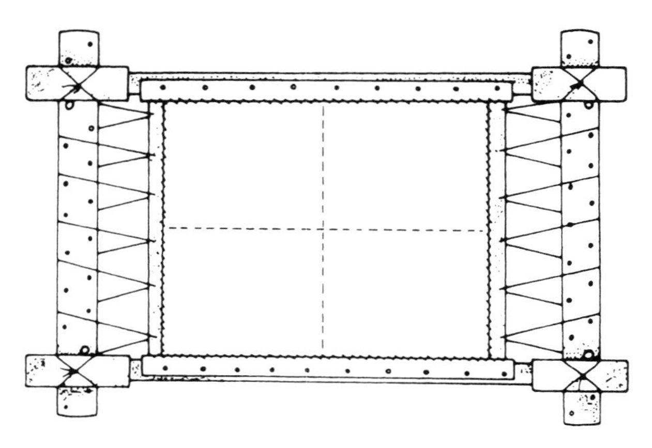

2 Insert the pegs or adjust the screw attachments to secure the frame. Thread a large-eyed needle (chenille needle) with strong thread or fine string and lace both edges, securing the ends around the intersections of the frame. Lace the webbing at 2.5cm (1in) intervals, stretching the fabric evenly.

MITRING A CORNER

Press a single hem to the wrong side, the same as the measurement given in the instructions. Open the hem out again and fold the corner of the fabric inwards as shown on the diagram. Refold the hem to the wrong side along the pressed line, and slipstitch in place.

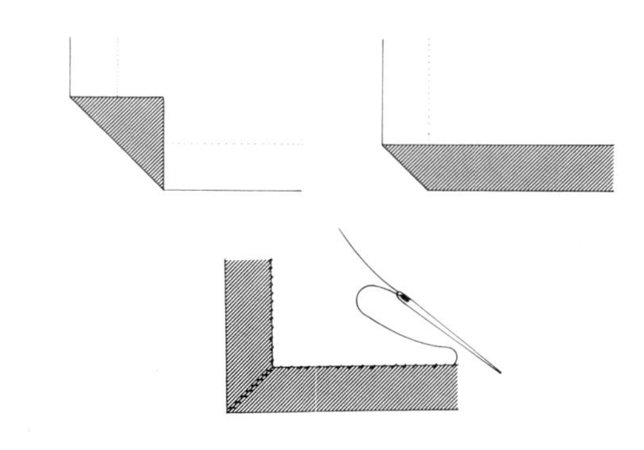

THE STITCHES

CROSS STITCH

For all cross stitch embroidery, the following two methods of working are used. In each case, neat rows of vertical stitches are produced on the back of the fabric.

• When stitching large areas, work in horizontal rows. Working from right to left, complete the first row of evenly spaced diagonal stitches over the number of threads specified in the project instructions. Then, working from left to right, repeat the

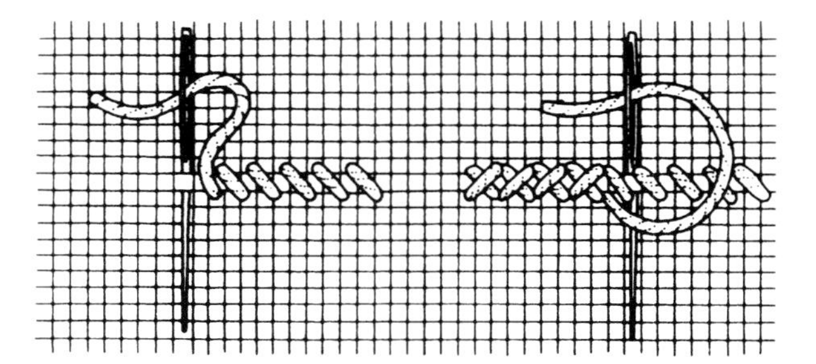

process. Continue in this way, making sure each stitch crosses in the same direction.

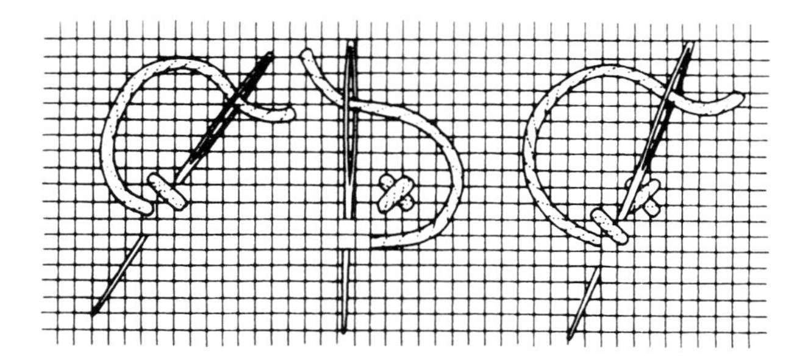

• When stitching diagonal lines, work downwards, completing each stitch before moving to the next. When starting a project, always begin to embroider at the centre of the design and work outwards to ensure that the design will be placed centrally on the fabric.

BACKSTITCH

Backstitch is used in the projects to give emphasis to a particular foldline, an outline or a shadow. The stitches are worked over the same number of threads as the cross stitch, forming continuous straight or diagonal lines.

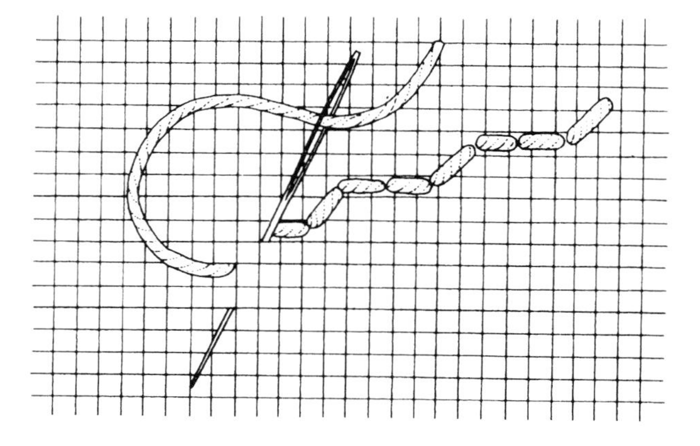

• Make the first stitch from left to right; pass the needle behind the fabric and bring it out one stitch length ahead to the left. Repeat and continue in this way along the line.

THREADING BLENDING FILAMENTS AND METALLIC THREADS

Both silky blending filaments and metallic braids are used in some of these projects. Some require the blending filament to be blended with stranded cotton while in others it is used singly. In each case, clear instructions are given in the text as to how many threads of each to use. For ease of working, slightly dampen the blending filament before knotting it into the needle and then threading on the stranded cotton. Metallic braids and blending filament should only be used in relatively short lengths to prevent tangling and to stop the fibres 'stripping' off as the thread is pulled through the fabric.

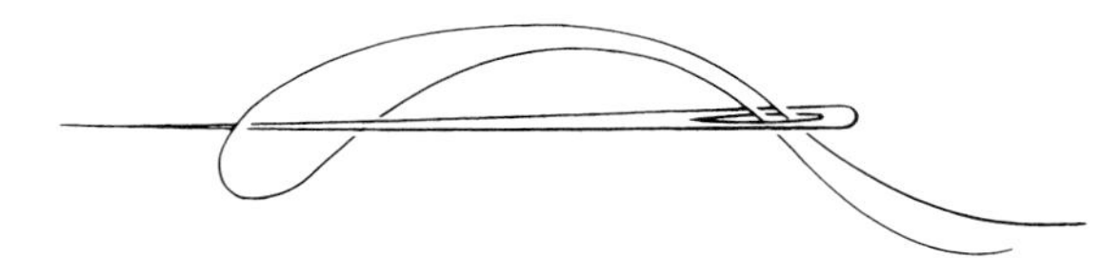

To thread blending filament, double the thread about 5cm (2in) at one end, and insert the loop through the eye of the needle. Pull the loop over the point of the needle and gently pull the loop towards the end of the eye to secure the thread to the needle. If you are using a combination of blending filament and stranded cotton, thread the latter through the eye in the usual way, and clip it to match the length of the blending filament.

USING PERFORATED PAPER

This may be purchased in A4-sized sheets in a variety of colours and is punched with holes; it will give you a finished piece of embroidery the same size as a piece stitched on 14-count Aida fabric. The holes are large to prevent tearing of the paper so three strands of embroidery thread should be used. Always cut your paper 5cm (2in) larger all round than your design to make it easier to handle.

A cross stitch is stitched between four of the holes on the paper. Handle the paper carefully when stitching, and pull the thread smoothly through the holes. If you tear the paper, however, it can be repaired with a small piece of sticky tape on the wrong side. If the chart you are using has been designed especially for perforated paper, it will include a cutting line, otherwise cut vertically, horizontally and diagonally around your embroidery when you have finished, making sure that you leave at least one square between the edge and your design so that the stitches do not come out.

FINISHING

MOUNTING EMBROIDERY

The cardboard should be cut to the size of the finished embroidery, with an extra amount added all round to allow for the recess in the frame.

LIGHTWEIGHT FABRICS

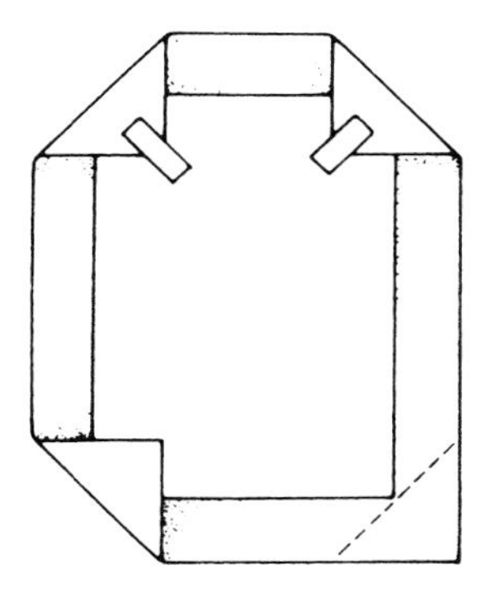

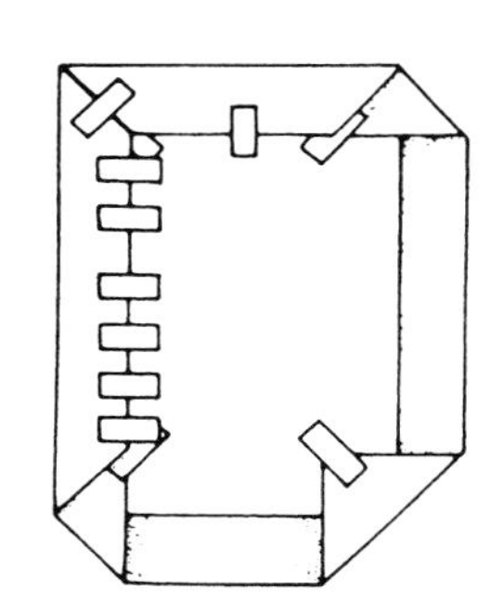

1 Place the embroidery face down, with the cardboard centred on top, and basting and pencil lines matching. Begin by folding over the fabric at each corner and securing it with masking tape.
2 Working first on one side and then the other, fold over the fabric on all sides and secure it firmly with pieces of masking tape which are placed about 2.5cm (1in) apart. Also neaten the mitred corners with masking tape, pulling the fabric tightly to give a firm, smooth finish.

HEAVIER FABRICS

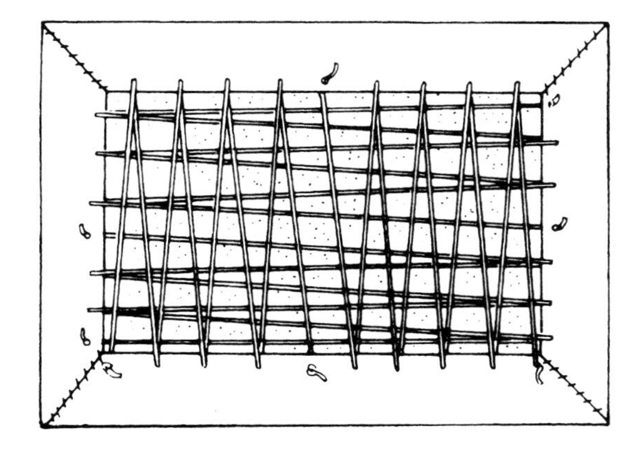

Lay the embroidery face down, with the cardboard centred on top; fold over the edges of the fabric on opposite sides, making mitred folds at the corners, and lace across, using strong thread. Repeat on the other two sides. Finally, pull up the fabric firmly over the cardboard. Overstitch the mitred corners.

Floral Bouquet

Worked on black evenweave linen for a dramatic effect, this bouquet of violets and lilies-of-the-valley uses beads and metallic threads to enhance the design. This challenging project is suitable for the more experienced stitcher.

FLORAL BOUQUET

YOU WILL NEED

For the Picture, with a design size measuring 16cm x 14cm (6³/8in x 5¹/2in):

25cm (10in) square of black, 28-count evenweave linen
Stranded embroidery cotton and specialist thread in the colours given in the panel
No24 tapestry needle
Seed beads in the colours given in the panel
Beading needle
Cardboard for mounting, sufficient to fit the frame recess
Strong thread for lacing across the back
Frame of your choice

•

THE EMBROIDERY

Prepare the fabric as explained on page 4. Find the centre and mark the horizontal and vertical lines with basting stitches, then mount the fabric in a frame. Start the embroidery at the centre of the design, using two strands of embroidery thread in the needle. When working the dark mauve stitches, use one strand of dark mauve thread and one strand of blending filament (see page 7). Work each stitch over two threads of fabric in each direction, ensuring that all the top crosses run in the same direction and that each row is worked into the same holes as the top or bottom of the row before so that you do not leave a space between the rows. Sew the beads in place as explained on this page.

FINISHING

Remove the finished embroidery from the frame and place it face down on a clean towel. Then gently steam press the work on the wrong side. Mount and frame the embroidery as explained on page 7.

ATTACHING BEADS

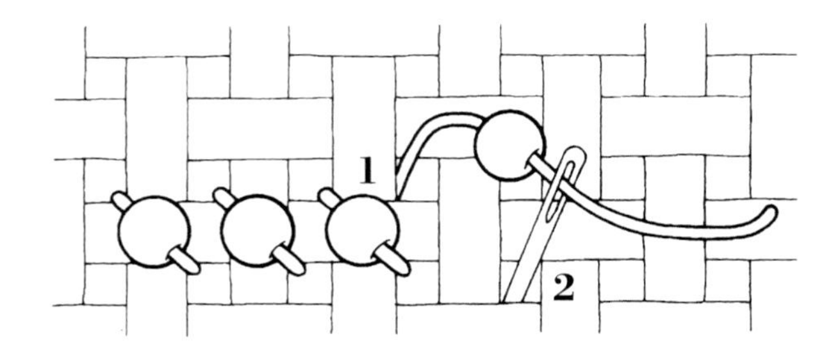

Refer to the chart for bead placement and sew the bead in place using a fine beading needle that will pass through the bead. Bring the needle up at 1, run the needle through the bead, then down at 2. Secure the thread on the back of the work, or move on to the next bead as shown in the diagram.

▶ **FLORAL BOUQUET**	DMC	ANCHOR	MADEIRA	KRE
◸ Grey	415	398	1803	
+ Light mauve	553	98	712	
⸌ Dark green	580	924	1608	
∃ Green	581	280	1609	
♥ Very dark green	731	281	1613	
◇ Light green	733	279	1611	
/ Dark mauve x 1 plus dark mauve blending filament x 1	3746	-	0804	
:: Navy blue beads	04.791	-	-	
– Yellow beads	06.307	-	-	
⊡ Pearl beads	10.blanc	-	-	

Note: One pack of beads in each colour is required.

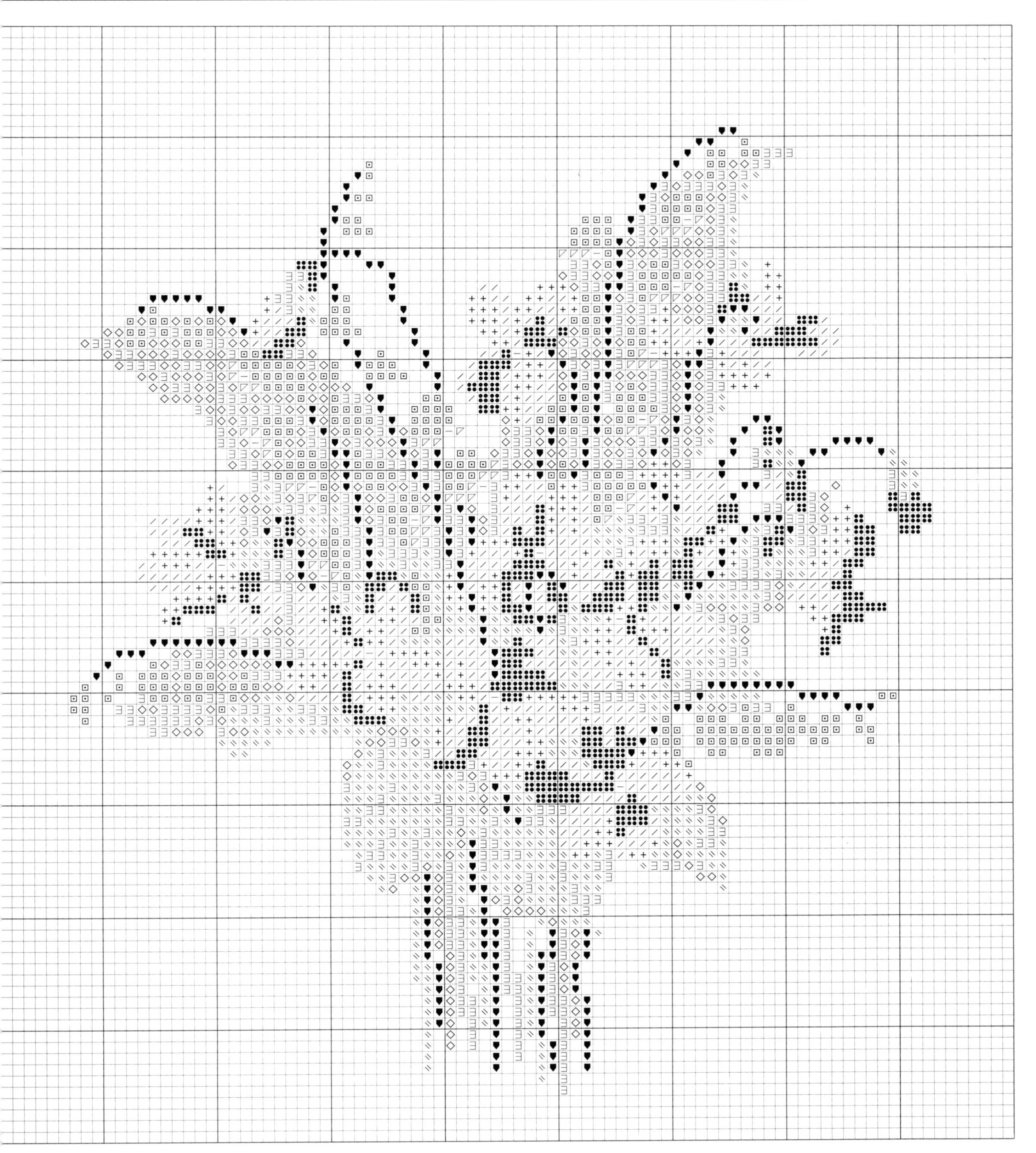

Birthday Greetings

Start your own collection of keepsakes by stitching these traditional-style cards on perforated paper which was a great favourite of the Victorians. If you feel they are too precious to give away, frame them and hang them on your wall.

BIRTHDAY GREETINGS

YOU WILL NEED

For the Pansy Bouquet Card, with a design size measuring 13cm x 10cm (5¼in x 4in):

16cm x 13cm (6⅜in x 5¼in) of stone-coloured perforated paper (shade SP004)
Stranded embroidery cotton and specialist thread in the colours given in the appropriate panel
No24 tapestry needle
Cream greetings card blank, 17.5cm x 13cm (7in x 5¼in) (for suppliers, see page 40)
Fabric glue

For the Forget-Me-Not Card, with a design size measuring 15cm x 9cm (6in x 3½in):

20cm x 15cm (8in x 6in) of stone-coloured perforated paper (shade SP004)
Stranded embroidery cotton and specialist thread in the colours given in the appropriate panel
No24 tapestry needle
Cream greetings card blank, 17.5cm x 13cm (7in x 5¼in) (for suppliers, see page 40)
Fabric glue

THE EMBROIDERY

Refer to the section on perforated paper on page 7 before starting the embroidery. Then, following the chart, begin the embroidery at the centre of the design, using three strands of thread in the needle for all parts of the design except for the gold or silver background, when you should use two strands of thread. Make sure that all cross stitches run in the same direction and that each row is worked into the same holes as the top or bottom of the row before so that you do not leave a space between the rows.

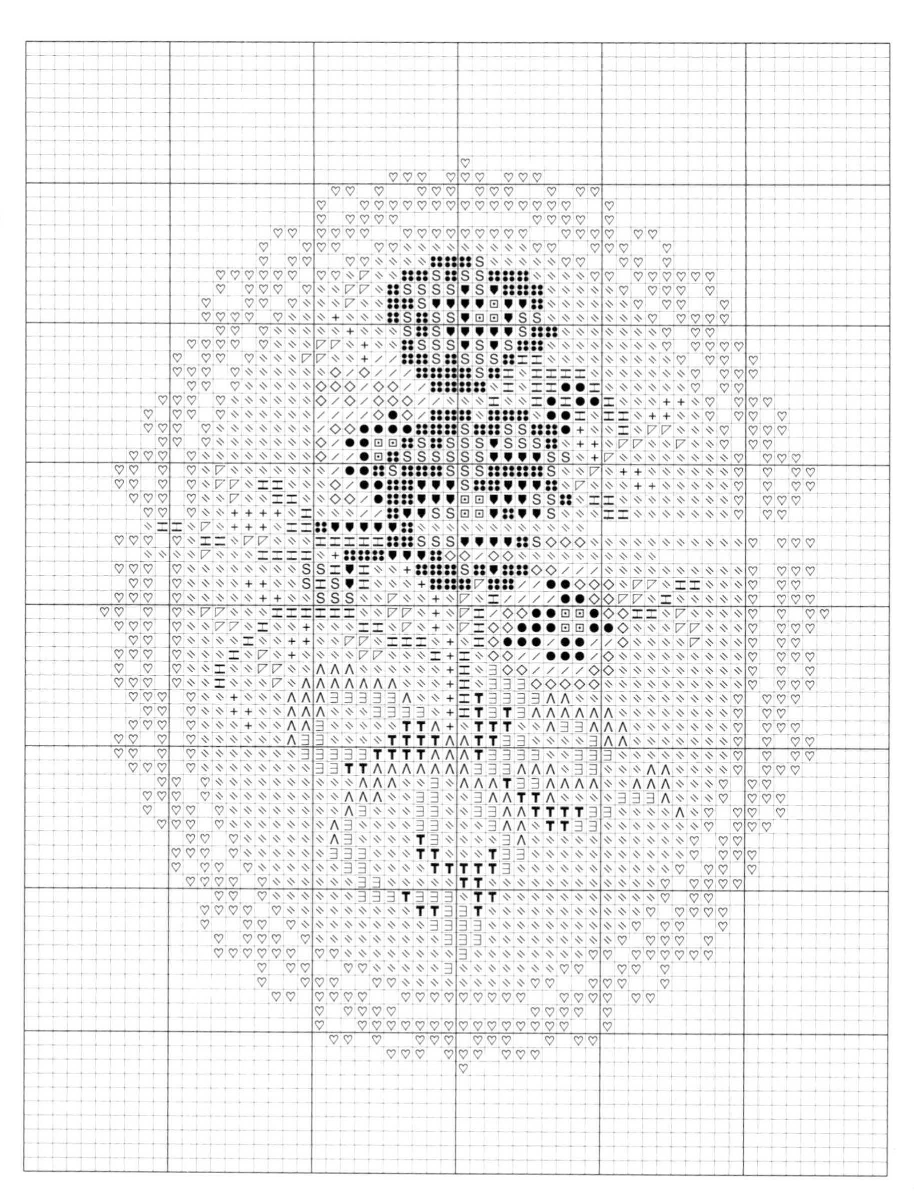

FINISHING

When you have completed the embroidery, carefully cut around the design leaving a border of two or three squares of paper. Spread fabric glue sparingly on the back of the embroidery and place it in the centre of a blank greetings card. Press down firmly and allow to dry.

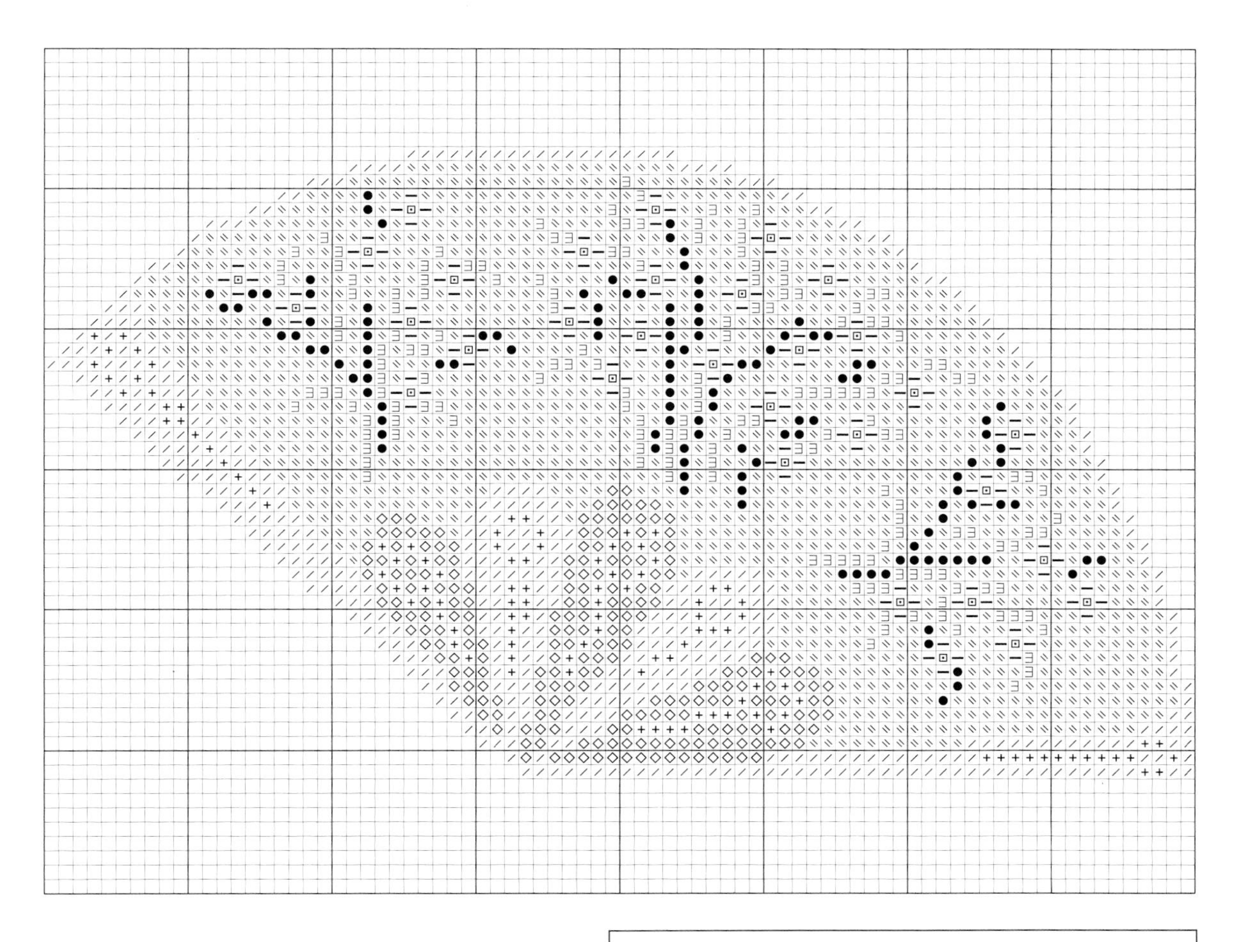

PANSY BOUQUET	DMC	ANCHOR	MADEIRA
Mauve	208	111	0712
Light mauve	210	108	0802
Brown	420	374	2104
Green	470	266	1503
Dark mauve	550	101	0714
Yellow	727	293	0103
Dark blue	798	131	0911
Blue	799	130	1910
Light blue	800	128	1002
Dark magenta	915	89	0705
Dark green	3345	268	1406
Light green	3348	264	1501
Magenta	3607	87	0708
Light magenta	3609	85	0710
Silver	D278.4041	-	-

▲ FORGET-ME-NOT CARD	DMC	ANCHOR	MADEIRA
⁄ Light brown	676	887	2208
+ Beige	677	300	2207
⊡ Yellow	727	293	0103
◇ Dark brown	729	890	2209
▬ Blue	799	130	0910
● Dark green	3347	266	1408
∃ Light green	3348	264	1501
⍀ Gold	D278.4042	-	-

Red Rose Cushion

The bold use of colour in this design of red roses on a navy blue background brings a traditional Berlin woolwork design right up to date, while still retaining the quality and feel of the original woolwork embroidery.

RED ROSE CUSHION

YOU WILL NEED

For the Cushion, with a design area measuring 15.5cm x 15cm (6¼in x 6in):

23cm (9in) square of navy blue, 14-count Aida fabric
Stranded embroidery cotton in the colours given in the panel
No24 tapestry needle
40cm (16in) square ready-made cushion cover
Pins
Matching sewing thread
45cm (18in) square cushion pad

●

THE EMBROIDERY

Prepare the fabric and stretch it in a frame as explained on page 4. Find the centre of the design and mark the central horizontal and vertical lines on the fabric with basting stitches. Following the chart, start the embroidery at the centre of the design using two strands of embroidery thread. Work each stitch over a block of fabric in each direction, making sure that all the top crosses run the same way and that each row is worked into the same holes as the row before.

FINISHING

Remove the finished embroidery from the frame and gently steam press it on the wrong side. Turn under 12mm (½in) on all sides of the embroidery, mitring the corners as explained on page 6. Centre the panel over the cushion cover, then pin and baste it into position. Appliqué the panel to the cover by slipstitching around the edge. Insert the cushion pad through the opening in the cover to complete.

▶ **RED ROSE CUSHION**	DMC	ANCHOR	MADEIRA
⁄ Light red	666	46	0510
⊡ Brown	729	890	2209
·|· Pink	892	28	0411
⌶ Dark green	905	258	1413
⑊ Green	906	256	1411
◇ Light green	907	255	1410
● Dark red	304	47	0511

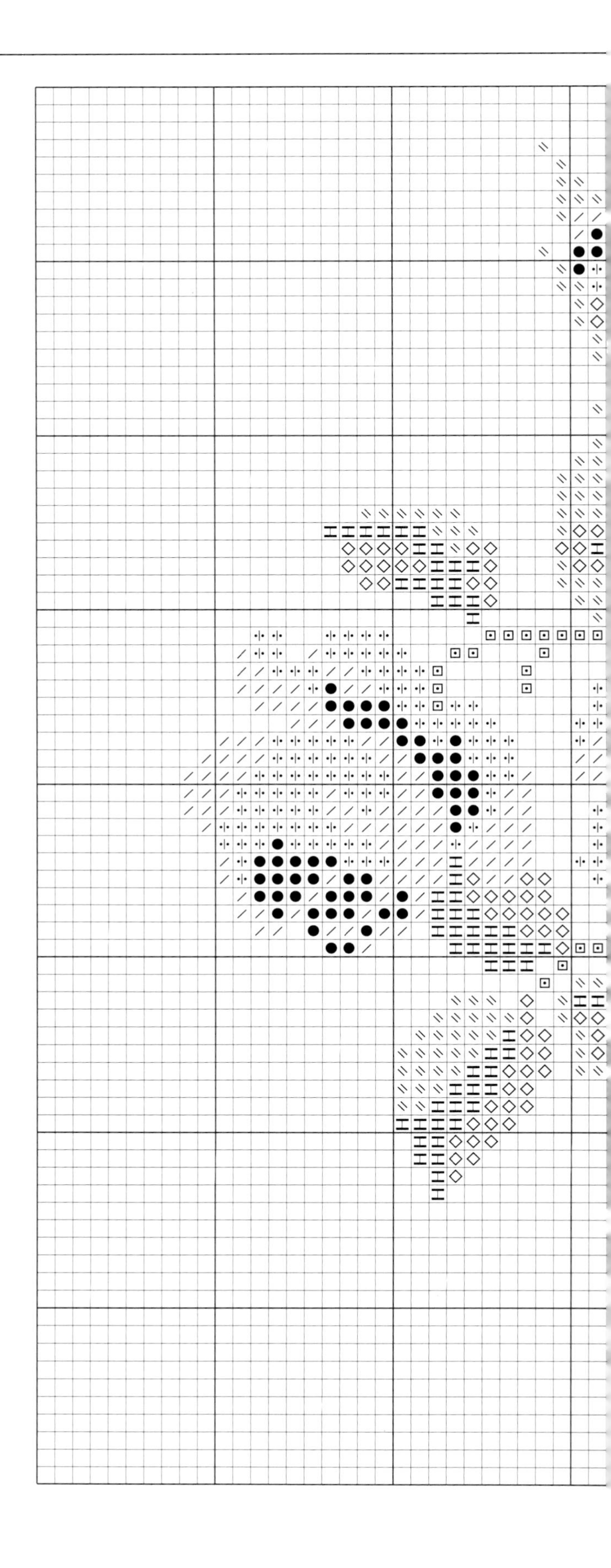

Floral Pictures

Bring a touch of old-fashioned elegance to your home with this charming trio of pansy, rosebud and marigold bouquets. Their beaded bows add extra decorative interest and carry on the tradition of Victorian embroidery.

FLORAL PICTURES

YOU WILL NEED

For the Pansy Picture, with a design size measuring 10cm x 8cm (4in x 3¼in):

20cm x 18cm (8in x 7¼in) of white, 26-count evenweave linen
Stranded embroidery cotton in the colours given in the appropriate panel
No24 tapestry needle
Seed beads in the colours given in the appropriate panel
Beading needle
Cardboard for mounting
Strong thread for lacing across the back
Frame of your choice

For the Rosebud Picture, with a design size measuring 10cm x 8cm (4in x 3¼in):

20cm x 18cm (8in x 7¼in) of white, 26-count evenweave linen
Stranded embroidery cotton in the colours given in the appropriate panel
No24 tapestry needle
Seed beads in the colours given in the appropriate panel
Beading needle
Cardboard for mounting
Strong thread for lacing across the back
Frame of your choice

For the Marigold Picture, with a design size measuring 11cm x 9cm (4⅜in x 3½in):

20cm x 18cm (8in x 7¼in) of white, 26-count evenweave linen
Stranded embroidery cotton in the colours given in the appropriate panel
No24 tapestry needle
Seed beads in the colours given in the appropriate panel
Beading needle
Cardboard for mounting
Strong thread for lacing across the back
Frame of your choice

THE EMBROIDERY

Prepare the fabric and stretch it in a hoop, as explained on page 4. Find the centre of the design and mark the central horizontal and vertical lines on the fabric with basting stitches. Following the correct chart, start the embroidery at the centre of the design, using two strands of embroidery thread in the needle. Work each cross stitch over two threads of fabric in each direction, ensuring that all the top crosses run in the same direction and that each row is worked into the same holes as the row before so that you do not leave a space between the rows. Work the backstitch using one strand of thread in the colour indicated in the panel. Sew the beads in place as explained on page 10.

FINISHING

Remove the embroidery from the hoop, place it face down on a clean towel and gently steam press. Mount and frame the embroidery as explained on page 7.

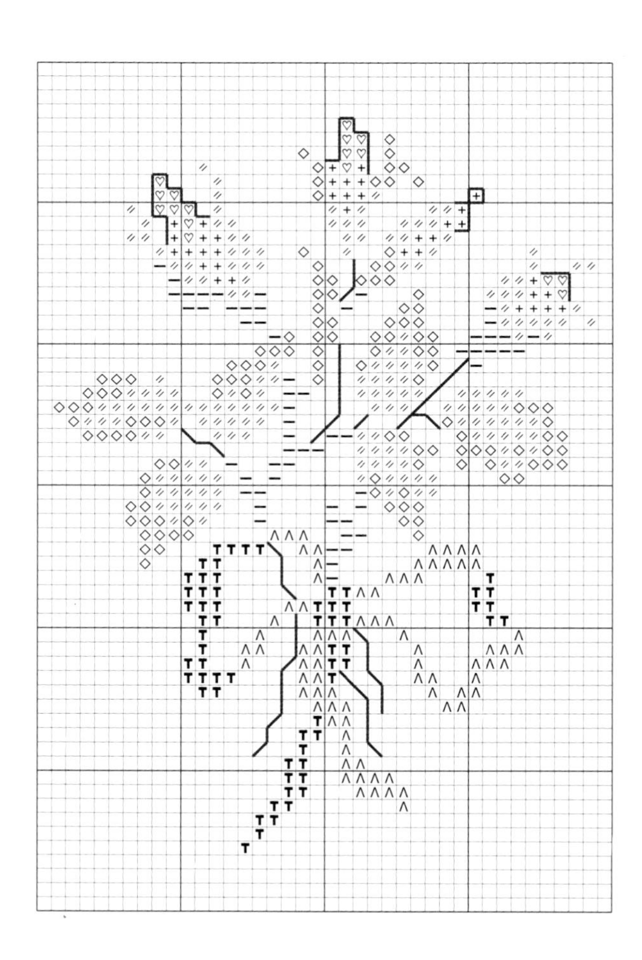

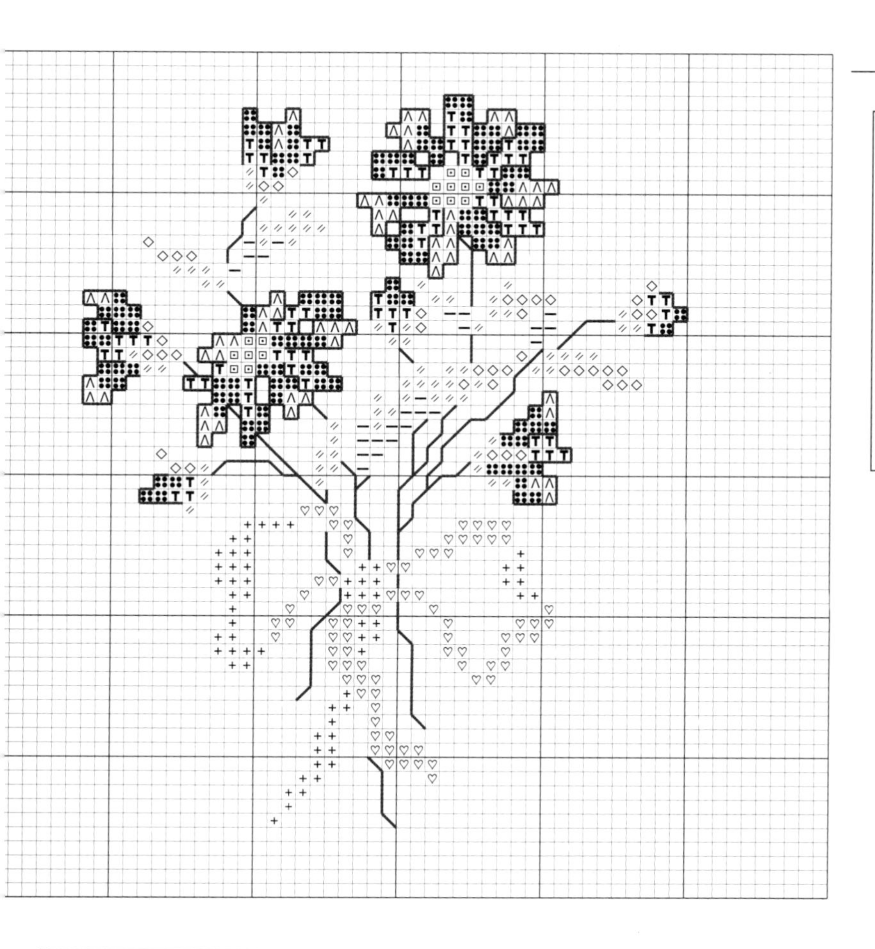

◀ MARIGOLD BOUQUET	DMC	ANCHOR	MADEIRA
⊡ Brown	435	363	2213
∧ Yellow	725	306	0108
T Dark orange	741	303	0201
:: Light orange	972	298	0114
▬ Dark green	3051	845	1514
⁄⁄ Green	3052	844	1502
◇ Light green	3348	264	1501
+ Gold beads	08.729	-	-
♡ Golden brown beads	09.676	-	-

Note: Backstitch flowers and stems in dark green. One pack of beads in each colour is required.

▶ PANSY BOUQUET	DMC	ANCHOR	MADEIRA
:: Mauve	340	118	0902
∧ Light mauve	341	117	0901
⊡ Yellow	727	293	0110
▬ Dark green	3051	845	1514
⁄⁄ Green	3052	844	1502
◇ Light green	3348	264	1501
T Dark mauve	3746	119	0903
+ Ice pink beads	01.818	-	-
♡ Pale pink beads	01.819	-	-

Note: Backstitch flowers and stems in dark green. One pack of beads in each colour is required.

◀ ROSEBUD BOUQUET	DMC	ANCHOR	MADEIRA
▬ Dark green	3051	845	1514
⁄⁄ Green	3052	844	1502
◇ Light green	3348	264	1501
+ Dark pink	3688	68	0605
♡ Light pink	3689	66	0613
∧ Lilac ice beads	05.3743	-	-
T Lilac beads	05.3746	-	-

ote: Backstitch flowers and stems in dark green. One pack of eads in each colour is required.

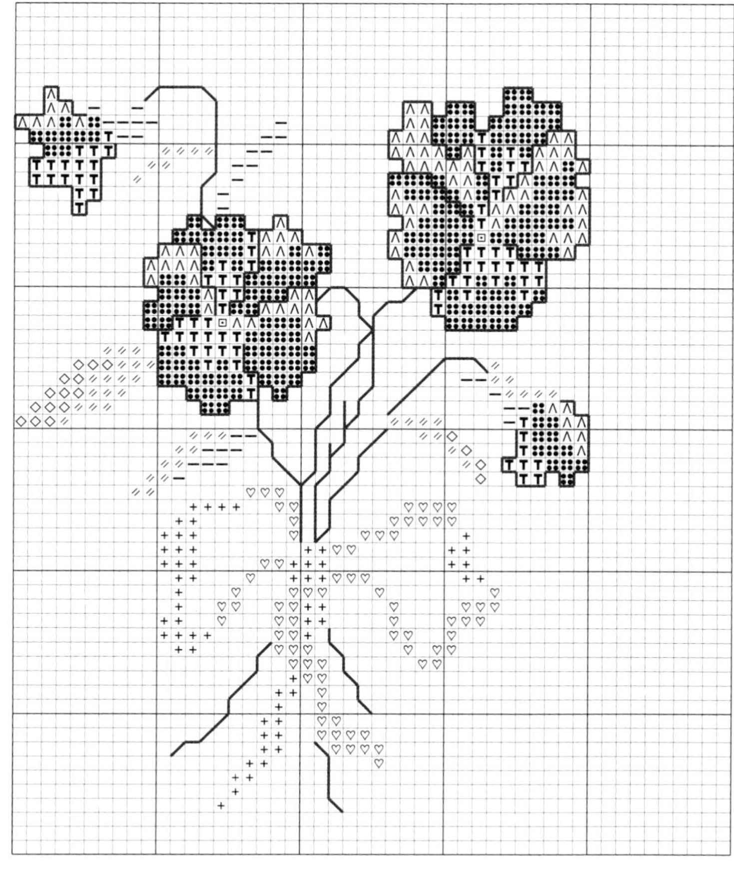

Golden Lace Fan

Emulate the Victorian era with this lace-effect fan, decorated with sprigs of violets and richly embellished with gold thread. This design is stitched on antique white Aida fabric, but you could use plastic canvas and trim it into a fan shape if you prefer.

GOLDEN LACE FAN

YOU WILL NEED

For the Picture, with a design size measuring 22.5cm x 14cm (9in x 5½in):

32.5cm x 24cm (13in x 9½in) of antique white, 14-count Aida fabric
Stranded embroidery cotton and specialist thread in the colours given in the panel
No24 tapestry needle
Cardboard for mounting, sufficient to fit the frame recess
Strong thread for lacing across the back
Mount and frame of your choice

•

THE EMBROIDERY

Prepare the fabric and stretch it in a frame as explained on page 4. Find the centre of the design and mark the central horizontal and vertical lines on the fabric with basting stitches. Following the chart, start the embroidery at the centre of the design using two strands of embroidery thread in the needle, except when using brown thread, when only one strand should be used. Work each cross stitch over one block of fabric in each direction. Make sure that all the top crosses run in the same direction and that each row is worked into the top or bottom of the row before so that you do not leave a space between the rows. Work the backstitch using one strand of thread in the needle.

FINISHING

Remove the completed embroidery from the frame, and wash, if necessary. Then place the embroidery face down on a clean towel, and gently steam press. Mount and frame the embroidery as explained on page 7.

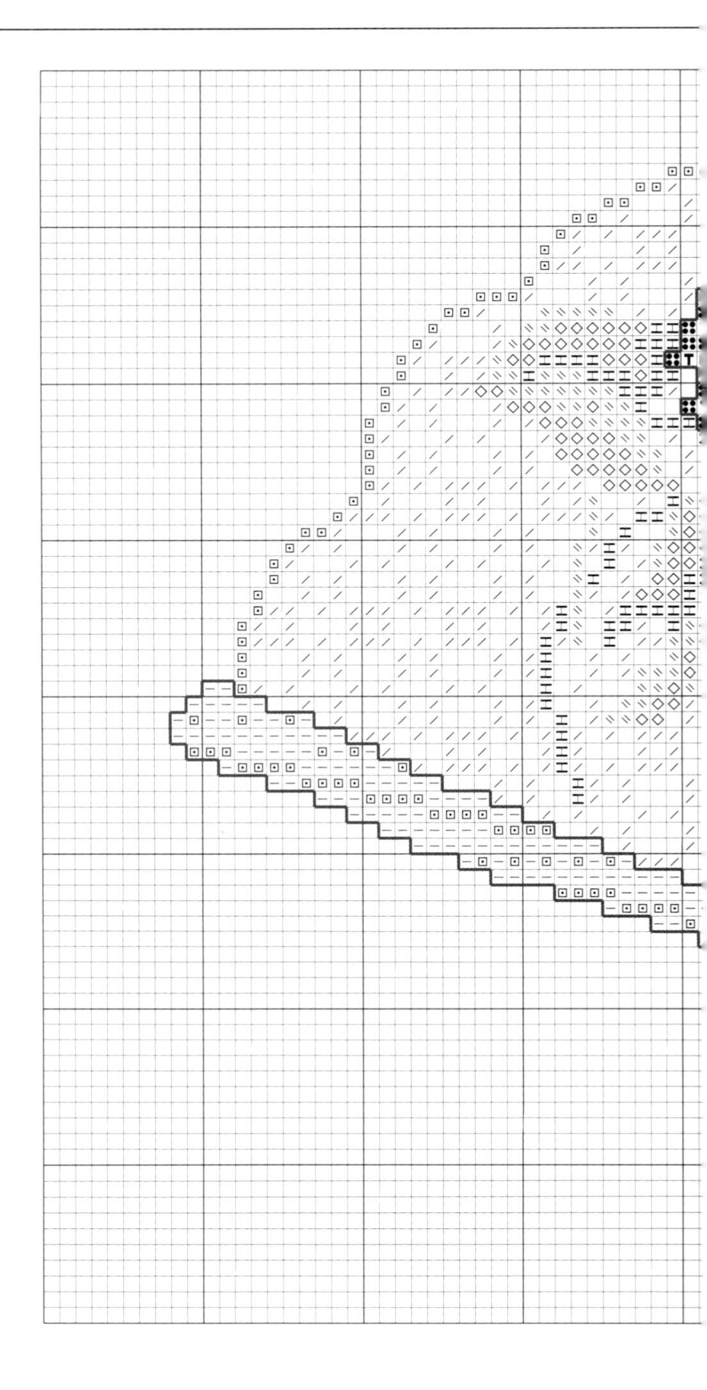

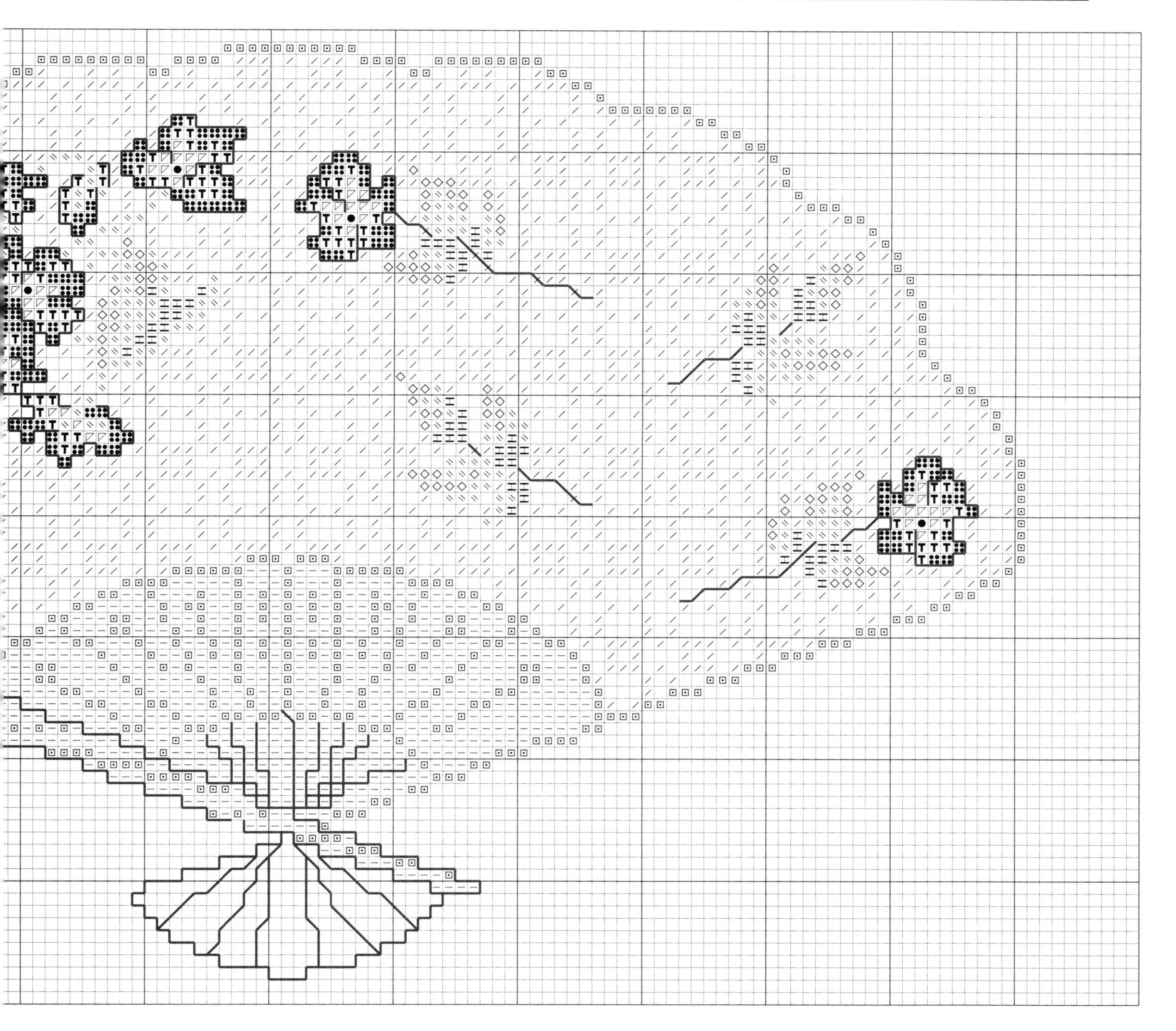

▲ LACE FAN	DMC	ANCHOR	MADEIRA
T Dark mauve	340	118	0902
⁘ Mauve	341	117	0901
● Yellow	727	293	0110
— Cream	746	275	2101
⁄ Brown (1 strand only)	841	378	1911
I Dark green	3345	268	1504
⸜ Green	3347	266	1502
◇ Light green	3348	264	1501
◸ Light mauve	3747	117	0901
⊡ Gold	4024	-	-

Note: Backstitch outlines in dark green.

Pot Pourri Delight

Enhance your bedroom with these rose fan designs for insertion into a crystal glass bowl, and the floral pot pourri sachets with their transparent inserts. Both designs are worked in a choice of two colourways to match your decor.

POT POURRI DELIGHT

YOU WILL NEED

For the Bowl Lid, with an insert measuring
9cm (3 1/2in) in diameter:

14cm (5 1/2in) square of white, 26-count evenweave linen
Stranded embroidery cotton in the colours given in the appropriate panel
No24 tapestry needle
Crystal bowl with prepared lid
(for suppliers, see page 40)

For the Pot Pourri Sachet, with a design size
measuring 15cm (6in) square:

20cm (8in) square of white, 26-count evenweave linen
Stranded embroidery cotton in the colours given in the appropriate panel
No24 tapestry needle
20cm (8in) square of fusible web
Fabric adhesive
10cm (4in) square of white muslin
20cm (8in) square of white cotton fabric
Matching sewing thread
Pot pourri of your choice
4 ribbon roses in a matching colour

●

THE BOWL

Prepare the fabric and stretch it in a hoop, as explained on page 4. Mark the central horizontal and vertical lines on the fabric with basting stitches. Following the correct chart, start stitching at the centre of the design using two strands of embroidery thread in the needle, except for the background of the fan which is worked in one strand. Work the cross stitch over two threads of fabric in each direction. Make sure that all the top crosses run in the same direction and that each row is worked into the top or bottom of the row before. Backstitch the base of the fan using one strand of thread, and backstitch the tassel using two strands.

Remove the finished embroidery from the hoop and steam press it. Assemble the bowl lid following the manufacturer's instructions.

THE POT-POURRI SACHET

Prepare the fabric and stretch it in a hoop as explained on page 4. Mark the central horizontal and vertical lines of the fabric with basting stitches. Following the correct chart, start at the centre of the design, using two strands of embroidery thread in the needle. Work the cross stitch over two threads of fabric in each direction. Work the backstitch with one strand of thread in the needle.

Remove the finished embroidery from the hoop and steam press it on the wrong side. Iron the square of fusible web on to the wrong side of the embroidery. Remove the backing paper and carefully cut a square of fabric from the centre of the embroidery, 12mm (1/2in) from the inside line of cross stitching. Apply fabric adhesive carefully around the edges of the opening on the wrong side and stick the square of muslin firmly in place. Allow to dry.

Place the embroidery and white cotton fabric together, right sides facing, and baste and machine stitch the two pieces of fabric together, 12mm (1/2in) away from the edge, leaving an opening of 5cm (2in) for turning. Trim the corners and turn the sachet very carefully to the right side. Fill with pot pourri then sew up the opening. Stitch a ribbon rose to each corner of the sachet to complete.

▶ **PINK ROSE FAN**	DMC	ANCHOR	MADEIRA
+ Light gold	745	386	0111
– Light gold (1 strand only)	745	386	0111
⌑ Dark pink	962	52	0505
⊡ Light pink	963	24	0607
T Dark green	3051	845	1508
∃ Green	3052	844	1509
◸ Light green	3348	264	1409
Λ Pink	3716	25	0606
■ Dark gold	3822	305	0110

Note: Backstitch base of fan in dark green; backstitch tassel thread in dark gold (2 strands).

▶ **YELLOW ROSE FAN**	DMC	ANCHOR	MADEIRA
⊡ Light yellow	727	293	0103
⌑ Dark yellow	742	302	0107
Λ Yellow	744	300	0110
+ Light gold	745	386	0111
– Light gold (1 strand only)	745	386	0111
T Dark green	3051	845	1508
∃ Green	3052	844	1509
◸ Light green	3348	264	1409
■ Dark gold	3822	305	0110

Note: Backstitch base of fan in dark green; backstitch tassel thread in dark gold (2 strands).

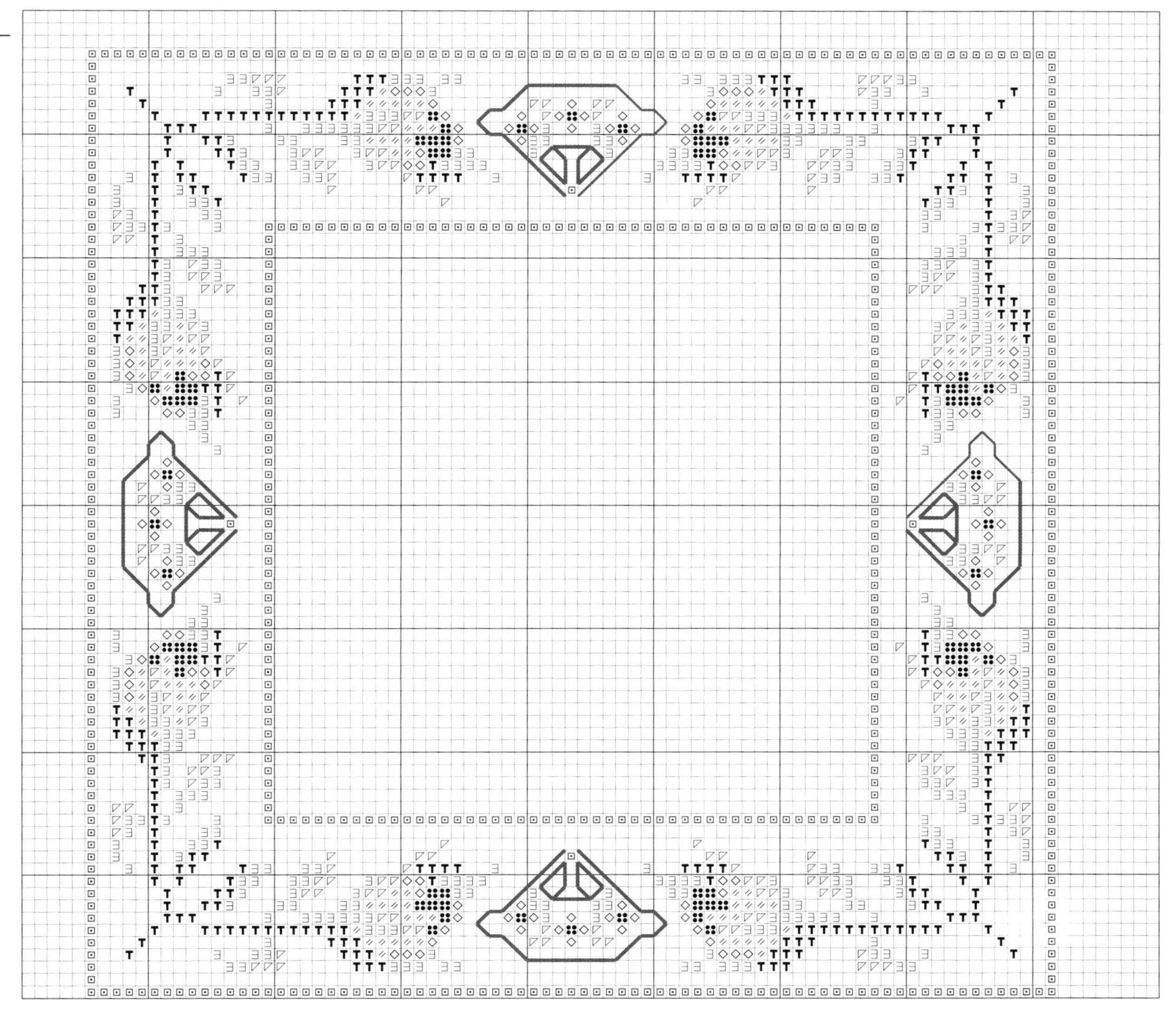

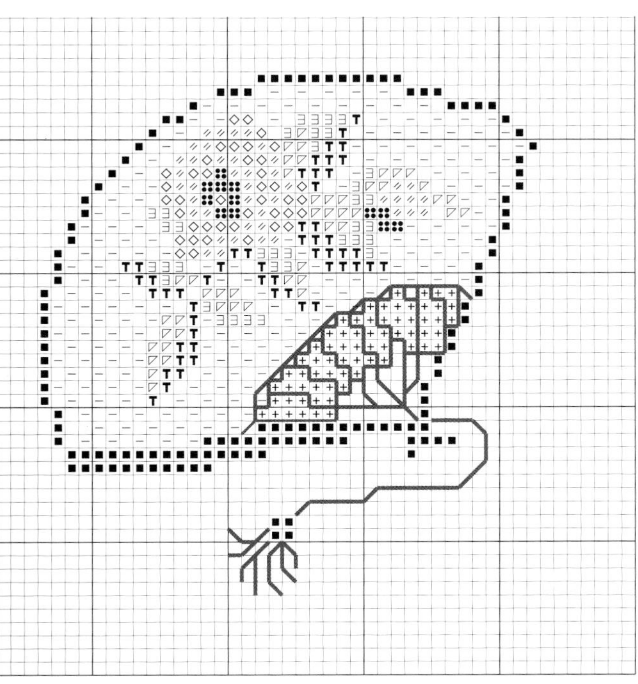

▲ PINK ROSE SACHET	DMC	ANCHOR	MADEIRA
∷ Dark pink	962	52	0505
◇ Light pink	963	24	0607
⁄⁄ Pink	3716	25	0606
T Dark green	3051	845	1508
∃ Green	3052	844	1509
◸ Light green	3348	264	1409
⊡ Dark gold	3822	305	0110

Note: Backstitch outlines in dark green.

▲ YELLOW ROSE SACHET	DMC	ANCHOR	MADEIRA
◇ Light yellow	727	293	0103
⁄⁄ Yellow	744	300	0110
∷ Dark yellow	742	302	0107
T Dark green	3051	845	1508
∃ Green	3052	844	1509
◸ Light green	3348	264	1409
⊡ Dark gold	3822	305	0110

Note: Backstitch outlines in dark green.

Miniature Studies

These exquisite miniatures in their elaborate frames and jewellery bases would compliment any outfit. Memories of great-grandmothers wearing high-necked dresses and beautiful jewellery are reflected in these designs.

MINIATURE STUDIES

YOU WILL NEED

For the Wreath Brooch, with a design size measuring 4cm (1½in) in diameter:

8cm (3¼in) square of antique white, 28-count evenweave linen
Stranded embroidery cotton in the colours given in the appropriate panel
No24 tapestry needle
Miniature jewellery frame for mounting the embroidery (for suppliers, see page 40)

For the Bouquet Brooch, with a design size measuring 4cm x 3cm (1½in x 1¼in):

8cm x 7cm (3¼in x 2¾in) of antique white, 28-count evenweave linen
Stranded embroidery cotton in the colours given in the appropriate panel
No24 tapestry needle
Miniature jewellery frame for mounting the embroidery (for suppliers, see page 40)

For the Rose Picture, with a design size measuring 4cm x 3cm (1½in x 1¼in):

8cm x 7cm (3¼in x 2¾in) of antique white, 28-count evenweave linen
Stranded embroidery cotton in the colours given in the appropriate panel
No24 tapestry needle
Miniature jewellery frame for mounting the embroidery (for suppliers, see page 40)

•

THE EMBROIDERY

Mark the centre of each piece of fabric with a vertical and horizontal line of basting stitches. As the fabric is so small, it is not necessary to mount it in a frame. Starting at the centre of the design, and using one strand of embroidery thread in the needle, work each cross stitch over one thread of fabric in each direction, following the chart. Work the backstitch on the Bouquet Brooch design with one strand of thread, as indicated in the key.

FINISHING

Steam press the completed embroidery gently on the wrong side, then mount the embroidery in the jewellery frame as explained in the manufacturer's instructions.

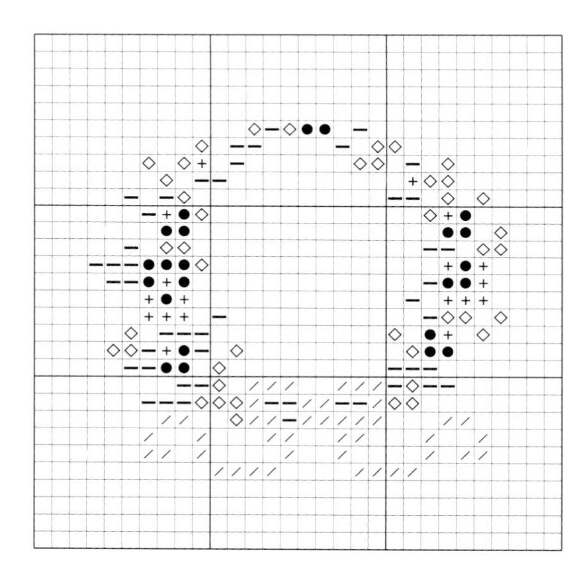

▲ WREATH	DMC	ANCHOR	MADEIRA
⁄ Mauve	208	111	0712
● Light pink	776	73	0606
+ Dark pink	899	40	0609
▬ Dark green	3347	266	1408
◇ Light green	3348	264	1501

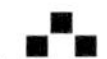

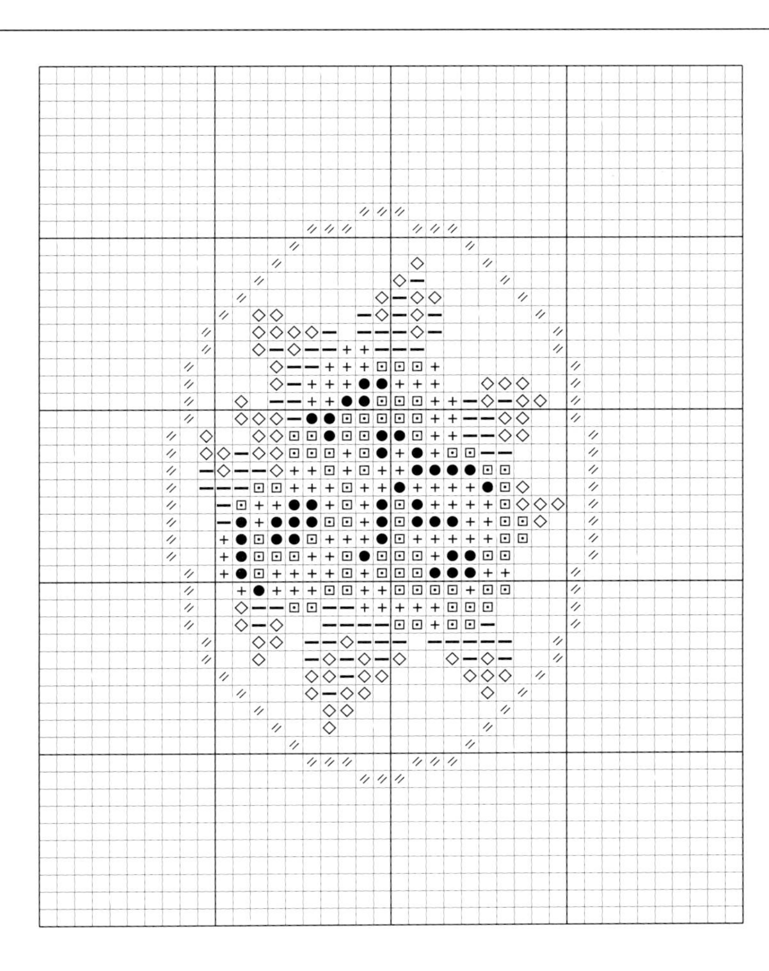

◀ ROSE PICTURE	DMC	ANCHOR	MADEIRA
● Dark red	304	47	0511
⁄⁄ Grey	415	398	1803
+ Light red	666	46	0510
⊡ Pink	892	28	0411
▬ Dark green	3347	266	1408
◇ Light green	3348	264	1501

▶ BOUQUET	DMC	ANCHOR	MADEIRA
⊡ Light pink	776	73	0606
⁄ Blue	798	131	0911
+ Pink	899	40	0609
▬ Dark green	3347	266	1408
◇ Light green	3348	264	1501
● Dark pink	3350	65	0603

Note: Backstitch stems in dark green.

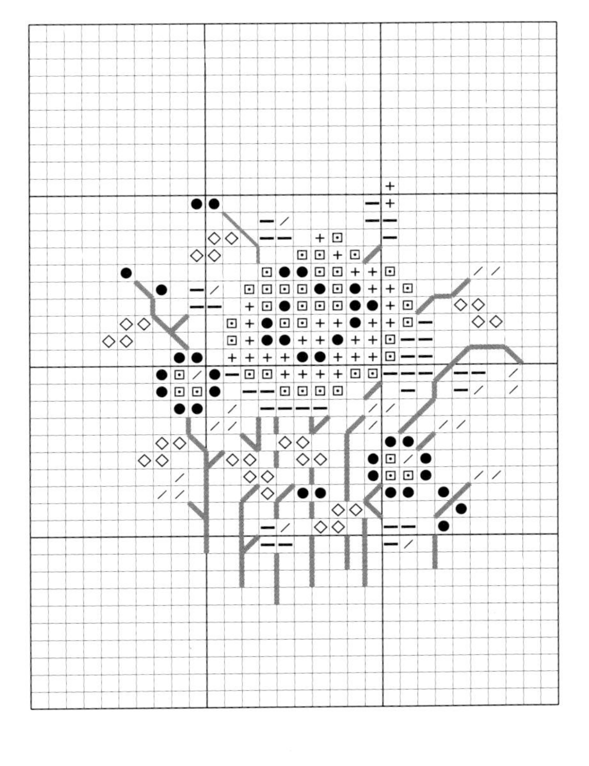

Pansy Spray Box

This richly embellished fan-shaped box, decorated with sparkling metallic threads and beads, would make a pretty gift for a special friend, or a future heirloom in which to store jewellery and other keepsakes.

PANSY SPRAY BOX

YOU WILL NEED

For the Pansy Box, with a design size measuring 15cm x 9cm (6in x 3½in):

22.5cm x 18cm (9in x 7¼in) of antique white, 14-count Aida fabric
Stranded embroidery cotton and specialist thread in the colours given in the panel
Size24 tapestry needle
Seed beads in the colours given in the panel
Beading needle
Fan box kit (for suppliers, see page 40)
22.5cm x 18cm (9in x 7¼in) of wadding
25cm (10in) square of pink felt
Fabric glue

•

THE EMBROIDERY

Prepare the fabric and mount it in a frame as explained on page 4. Mark the central horizontal and vertical lines on the fabric with basting stitches. Following the chart, start the embroidery in the centre of the design, using two strands of embroidery thread in the needle. Embroider the areas of stranded cotton first, working each cross stitch over one block of fabric in each direction. Then embroider the areas of metallic thread, using two strands of thread as before (see page 7 for tips on working with metallic thread). Work the backstitch using two strands of metallic cotton. Sew the pink and gold beads in place as explained on page 10.

FINISHING

Remove the embroidery from the frame and place it face down on a thick towel. Then gently steam press it. Cover the box with wadding and pink felt, securing it with fabric glue, then assemble the box as explained in the manufacturer's instructions.

▶ **PANSY SPRAY**	DMC	ANCHOR	MADEIRA	KREINIK
∷ Dark pink	815	22	0512	-
◸ Pink	3804	63	0703	-
⁄⁄ Light pink	3806	60	0701	-
Gold blending filament*	-	-	-	002
+ Green blending filament	-	-	-	008
▬ Dark green blending filament*	-	-	-	009
◇ Light green blending filament	-	-	-	015
⊡ Antique gold beads	V2.08.3820	-	-	-
S Shocking pink beads	V3.01.917	-	-	-

Note: Backstitch fan edge and honeycomb pattern at base of fan in gold blending filament; backstitch flower stems in dark green blending filament* (*used for backstitch only). One spool of blending filament in each colour, and one packet of beads in each colour are required.*

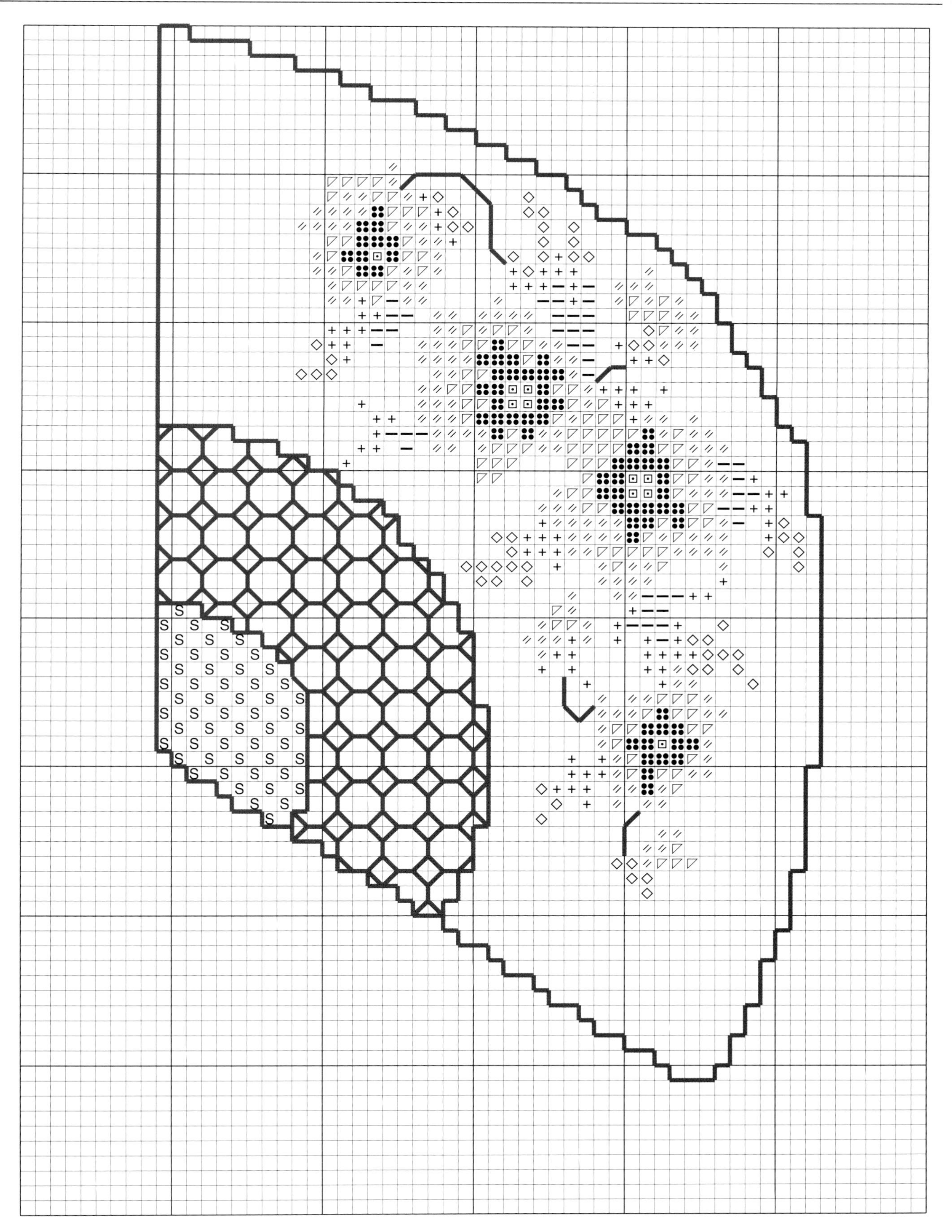

ACKNOWLEDGEMENTS

The author would like to thank the following people for their help with the projects in this book: Phoebe Spooner, Angela Hardy and especially Helen Burke.

Thanks are also due to: DMC Creative World Ltd for supplying fabric, beads, threads and mounting board; Framecraft Miniatures Ltd for supplying the crystal bowl; Hanging by a Thread for supplying the fan box kit; Elizabeth R Anderson for supplying the miniatures; and Fabric Flair for supplying fabric and perforated paper.

Enquiries about embroidery kits designed by Jane Alford under the Reflexions and Cross Purposes label may be sent to Richard and Jane Alford, Reflexions/Cross Purposes, The Stables, Black Bull Yard, Welton, Lincoln LN2 3HZ.

SUPPLIERS

Miniatures for embroidery (page 32):
Elizabeth R Anderson
Rosedale, 16 Tall Elms
Close, Bromley
Kent BR2 0TT
Telephone: 0181-460 1951

Fabric and perforated paper (page 12):
Fabric Flair Ltd
Unit 3 Northlands
Industrial Estate
Copheap Lane, Warminster
Wiltshire BA12 0BG
Telephone: 0800 716851

Fan box kit (page 36):
Hanging by a Thread
PO Box 10723
London SE3 02L
Telephone: 0181-318 3185

Greetings card blanks (page 12):
Impress Cards and Craft
Materials, Slough Farm,
Westhall, Halesworth
Suffolk IP19 8RN

Crystal bowl (page 28):
FRAMECRAFT
Framecraft Miniatures Ltd
372-376 Summer Lane
Hockley
Birmingham B19 3QA
Telephone : 0121-359 4442

Addresses for Framecraft stockists worldwide

Ireland Needlecraft Pty Ltd
PO Box 1175
Narre Warren M.D.C.
Victoria 3805
Australia

Danish Art Needlework
PO Box 442,
Lethbridge
Alberta T1J 3Z1
Canada

Sanyei Imports
PO Box 5,
Hashima Shi
Gifu 501-62
Japan

The Embroidery Shop
286 Queen Street
Masterton
New Zealand

Anne Brinkley Designs Inc.
246 Walnut Street
Newton
Mass. 02160
USA

S A Threads and
Cottons Ltd
43 Somerset Road
Cape Town
South Africa

For more information on your nearest stockist of embroidery cotton, contact the following:

DMC
(also distributors of Zweigart fabrics)
UK
DMC Creative World Ltd
62 Pullman Road, Wigston
Leicester LE8 2DY
Telephone: 0116 2811040

USA
The DMC Corporation
Port Kearney, Building 10
South Kearney
N.J. 07032
Telephone: 201 589 0606

AUSTRALIA
DMC (Australia) Pty Ltd
PO Box 317
Earlwood
NSW 2206
Telephone: 02 9559 3088

COATS AND ANCHOR
UK
Coats Paton Crafts
McMullen Road
Darlington
Co. Durham DL1 1YQ
Telephone: 01325 381010

USA
Coats & Clark
PO Box 24998
Dept COI
Greenville SC 29616
Telephone: 800 243 0810

AUSTRALIA
Coats Spencer Crafts
Private Bag 15
Mulgrave North
Victoria 3181
Telephone: 03 9561 2288

MADEIRA
UK
Madeira Threads (UK) Ltd
Thirsk Industrial Park
York Road
Thirsk
North Yorkshire YO7 3BX
Telephone: 01845 524880

USA
Madeira Marketing Ltd
600 East 9th Street
Michigan City
IN 46360
Telephone: 219 873 1000

AUSTRALIA
Penguin Threads Pty Ltd
25-27 Izett Street
Prahran
Victoria 3181
Telephone: 03 9529 4400